HOW TO START

A

MARIJUANA
INVESTMENT CLUB

By Mickey Dee

Frazier Publishing & Services
P. O. Box 363835
North Las Vegas, NV 89036

This book is dedicated to my family and friends who make my life so much better. God bless you!

This book is not intended for use as a source of legal, business, accounting of financial advice. All readers are advised to seek services of competent professionals in their respective fields.

TABLE OF CONTENTS

INTRODUCTION

This book is designed to provide all the information regarding a Marijuana Investment Club, including how to join one, start one and keep it running effectively forever.

You will be in a position to start your own Marijuana Investment Club after reading this book and carefully following the steps outlined here. There are numerous investment clubs around the country that have been running for a number of years. With a little effort and planning you too can be part of a successful Marijuana Investment Club.

After reading this book you will learn the following:

- What a marijuana investment club is all about

- The excitement of investing

- Why you should start an investment club

- Personal reasons for starting a marijuana investment club

- Features that should be present in both the marijuana investment club and its members

- The various types of investors and traders

- How many members you will need

- How to get members for a marijuana investment club

- Why a marijuana investment club can better your life

- What to anticipate from the first meeting

- What types of officials to elect for the club

- Different types of business models

- How to register your marijuana investment club

- The significance of a mission statement

- The significance of an education program

- Types of agents

- Types of investment software

- Resources for marijuana investment clubs

- The most active marijuana stocks in the present day

- The significance of stock symbols

- A glossary of investing terms

This book will get you up and investing in no time and can be used as a guideline for successfully joining or starting your own investment club.

The important thing is to have fun investing and learning about the stock market with a group of people that share your interests.

WHAT ABOUT A MARIJUANA INVESTMENT CLUB?

An investment club is basically a group of individuals with a common interest in the stock market pooling their resources into one large investment. Describing how a marijuana investment club functions is more intricate.

In most instances, the marijuana investment club will be registered as a corporation and the members of the club will make decisions together on what stocks or etf's they consider to be a worthy investment possibility. Most of the time, decisions regarding the investment will be made after some research has been conducted regarding the stock under consideration. This will be discussed at length in this book along with specific marijuana stocks.

A significant feature of an investment club is that the members are there to have fun as they invest their money and learn about the stock market. Making a profit isn't the only goal of the club and members are encouraged to have fun and learn as they invest their money.

A marijuana investment club is not for those individuals who are looking for a fast way to make some easy money. Individuals want a quick turn-around are not fit to join an investment group and invest on their own.

A key feature of the investment group is learning how to invest one's money and to invest for a long-term rather than a short-term. However, It's important to remember investing is a marathon and not a sprint so you have the rest of your life.

There are some things that you should note down if you are considering starting an investment club or interested in joining one that already exists.

Ensure that you comprehend all the reasons why you should start an investment club and the requirements necessary to be successful as a club. The following is a list of key ideas and information that you should consider before starting your club:

Be realistic. If you are starting an investment club to make a killing in the stock market, you will most likely be very dissatisfied. The aim of a marijuana investment club is to learn more regarding the stock market and if you have a vision of becoming wealthy you will be starting the club for the wrong reasons. Joining any investment club means joining for a long period of time. There are investment clubs that have made millions as they have grown their portfolio over the long haul.

1. *You're not expected to be an expert.* Starting an investment club does not imply that you have to be skilled in the stock market. Act, As a matter of fact, an investment club is perfect for a group of amateurs who want to learn how the stock market functions and what it can offer them. An investment club is a secure environment in which you can invest a small amount of money and not worry about losing a large amount of your hard earned money when something sudden transpires. One of the big benefits ism people from all walks of life share their knowledge and expertise.

2. *Amount of capital to invest and when*: one does not need a large amount of money to start an investment club. You can set a small fee for each month's contribution that is fits into your budget. Maybe your investment club decides to contribute quarterly. You will have the opportunity to decide what the minimum monthly contribution should be when you have your first meeting of the investment club.

Funds pooled together. A single person may not have enough money to invest in the stock market in a way in which one may be able to get returns. Though, when you pool your investment money with the others in the club, you will have a substantial amount of capital to invest in the stock market that you have been observing and think may be successful. Keep in mind that just as there is power in numbers there is also a collective sense of confidence when you are not investing alone.

3. *Diplomacy.* You should keep in mind that your opinion will be part of the larger group, and you may not always have a choice in the stock you want to invest in. If you are not able to sit back and let another decision take the place of something that you

would rather see, then an investment club might not be for you. You will need to be in a position to let the majority rule whenever a decision is made.

4. *Learning experience.* One should be ready to be content to never realize returns from the stock market. One of the main objectives and characteristics of an investment club is that you benefit from the learning experience of being with other people who have a common interest in the stock market. If you never get returns, you should still be contented with your involvement as part of an investment group.

After the market went through a bear bottoming process in the 1990's, the market has seen blue skies breakouts with a hiccup here and there.

VIX® Index and S&P 500® (SPX) Index Since 1990

Daily closing values. (Jan. 1990 - Feb. 8, 2018) The VIX index is not investable.
Sources: Bloomberg and Cboe   www.cboe.com/VIX

8

Starting your own marijuana investment club will be a pleasurable, and possibly profitable, as you spend time with other people with similar investment passion as you.

You will be able to gain experience concerning the stock market in a safe and secure environment with other individuals that understand your interest in the stock market.

The Marijuana Investing Thrill

Investing in the stock market is an enjoyable and thrilling way to learn more regarding financing and more about investing your capital effectively. When you start observing the stock market, you will see stock prices fall radically overnight or jump extremely into a crazy arc of profit.

This ecstasy can be thrilling and great but you have to decide if this type of risk taking with your hard earned money is something that you want to participate in or watch from a distance.

You need to be very conscious of the fact that you might lose the money that you have invested overnight. If your objective for your finances is to save money securely so that you can retire, then maybe you need to put your money into a savings account and watch it grow gradually.

Although, if you are ready to take risks so that your money has the possibility to grow fast and in large amounts, then you have the impeccable character for someone who should be part of an investment club.

YESTERDAY, TODAY and TOMORROW Your Money will show steady growth if you stay the course in the stock market!!

Individuals who are part of an investment club are ready to take risks so that they can make a profit, appreciating the whole process of the stock market and checking every day to see how their stocks have done overnight.

However, they are also sane and coherent when it comes to their money, wanting to stop working with a nice sized nest egg as a cushion.

Capitalizing in the stock market is one way that you can make a large amount of money while having pleasure doing so. When you capitalize in the stock market you have to be ready to have some instances where you are working at a loss. During those instances when the stock market is sluggish you are possibly better off putting your money into a savings account in the bank.

However, if you are persistent and ride out the sluggish times of the stock market you will come back with a bang and make more returns than if you had essentially put your money into a savings account.

When you are part of an investment group, you are pooling your money with other investors who tolerantly wait through the sluggish times of the market for your investment returns to pick up again.

There are some good reasons why capitalizing in the stock market is both sensible and lucrative:

1. You have the opportunity for much better results and returns compared to when you invest your capital in pension savings or into the bank. Your capital will be much more "liquid", implying that you are in a

position to move it around in the stock market which you might not be able to do if you lock your money into a savings account. This does not imply that you want to continuously purchase and trade your stock. However, it means that you will have more control over where your capital goes, what you do with it, and how much of the money you want to invest into the stock market.

2. When you capitalize in the stock market, you will have assortment with your savings and capital that you acquire from other sources, such as inherited money, assurance, real estate, or your business undertakings. If you have spare money that is not spoken for by bills and other expenditures, you will want to consider investing your money.

3. You are in a position to realize some visions in your life that you may not be able to meet if you did not have the revenue that you can make from investing. Playing the stock market implies taking some of your ideas and making them an actuality.

4. You will become much more informed regarding the investing and corporate environment. If you are already interested in capital investment, then being part of an investment club is an ideal way to gain more understanding and share your similar interests with other people. You will be in a position to get together on a regular basis with people who are learning about the stock market right beside you.

5. When you capitalize in the stock market, you are taking your assets into your own control. You are not relying on the government for your future financial necessities.

Always remember that you might never see significant returns for a long time. This should not disappoint you; instead, it should motivate you as you do something that captivates you.

My Reasons for Starting a Club

Now that you know the delight and pleasure that investing in the stock market can bring to your life, you will want to know some of the reasons why people start investment clubs. These reasons include:

- *Joint investment knowledge.* When you work with a group of individuals with similar interests in the stock market, you will be able to have a huge amount of collective knowledge working in your favor. Even those complete beginners in the stock market will have a treasured view and bits of information that when you sum it all together translates to a lot of thinking power. As long as you have a strategy of diplomacy, you will be able to make decisions regarding where you are going to invest your capital in such a manner as the decision is of the majority and is established on a great deal of thought. If you are not able to take direction from a group of individuals that you are working with then an investment club may not be for you. Do not let the tough guidelines; articles of association or investment risk turn you away.

- *Personal risk is low.* Although the capital that your club has to invest can be somewhat large, your own personal input can be very negligible. This way you avoid risking much of your money while you study how the stock market functions. You can still make some large investments but your loss factor will be adaptable for you. Remember that when your club makes a profit, no matter how trivial, the amount must be distributed among all the members.

- *More room for revenue.* Contemporary studies of investment clubs indicate that when a group of individuals make investment resolutions after a sequence of consultations and considerations, the possibility for profit is more than when individuals make their own resolutions regarding where and how to invest their capital.

16

- *Mutual interests*. Members of an investment club appreciate coming together on a regular basis to discuss the investment market and to learn more regarding a subject that greatly benefits them.

- *Invest frequently*. Investment clubs are able to invest in the stock market even when the market is falling or is sluggish. Since the capital is distributed among a group of members, the room for huge personal loss does not exist.

- *Re-invest*. Since majority of the members are part of an investment club for pleasure, and to learn more about the stock market, there will be more room for re-investing the returns and bonuses that are earned from prosperous investments. When you invest on your own you will not be ready to part with earned investment capital and re-invest everything that you gain.

- *Distribute investments*. When you are investing with a group of individuals you can spread your investments and not limit yourself to just one or two market selections. With a marijuana investment

17

group you will avoid the tendency to put all your money in one basket that may have holes in it. Marijuana and cannabis companies will include agricultural companies, food companies, wellness companies, beverage companies and many more. Marijuana Electronic Trading Funds (ETF's) will play a major role in diversification.

There are a number of other causes why it's equally valuable for people to join together in an investment club. The key reason is that individuals have a sincere interest in sharing their investment involvement and knowledge with others with similar interests.

PERSONAL REASONS FOR JOINING A MARIJUANA INVESTMENT CLUB

There are private reasons that you will want to start or join an investment club. You will ultimately have the chance to play the stock market in a secure environment that is low risk and allows you learn more regarding a topic that greatly interests you.

Personal reasons for joining an investment club include:

- *Assurance*. You might feel safer and more confident when you learn about the investment world with a group of other individuals with the same interests.

- *Starting out*. If you have constantly wanted to capitalize in the stock market but been hesitant to lose huge amounts of money because you don't know what you are doing, then an investment club is ideal

19

for you because you can be part of a large investment crew.

- *Low investments.* If you only have less capital to invest every month, such as $25 to $60 dollars, then an investment club is ideal for you. You can invest small amounts of capital into the larger combined total of the whole club.

- *Investing education.* If you have always desired to learn more regarding investing in the stock market, but you keep putting your desire aside, an investment club is a perfect way to motivate you to show up in meetings and learn more about investment.

- *Socializing.* Coming together with a group of individuals with the same interests is a gratifying way to learn about something that you have always wanted to be informed about.

- *Motivation.* When you can safely work with individuals with mutual interests you will be encouraged to take risks and learn as much as you can about investing.

There are lots of other causes why you should start or join an investment club. The main thing is that you want to invest some of your capital in a way that is exciting and informative.

REQUIREMENTS OF A SUCCESSFUL MARIJUANA INVESTMENT CLUB

For an investment club to be prosperous, there are a number of requirements which must be in place so that the club functions efficiently. When a group of persons come together with common interests, they need to have definite conditions that are met and basic guidelines that are followed.

Each member of the club needs to be sure of the anticipations and needs to have some simple attributes that are met.

Some of these requirements include:

- *Investment objectives.* Every member of the club needs to have the same objective in mind and the same techniques of accomplishing that objective. If some members of the club are only concerned with making a profit; rather than learning more regarding investing and the specifics involved, there will be a divided set of objectives. All members of the club should have the same viewpoint about investing.

- *Long-term objectives.* Members of the group should be clear on what the long-term objectives of the club are all about. There should be an understanding established of what amount of the revenue that is acquired from investment is going to be held and which amount is going to be re-invested instantly back into the stock market. There should be an equivalent amount of growth and constancy that is decided upon.

- *Systematized communication.* Group members should communicate on a regular basis. Part of the experience of starting an investment club is getting together to appreciate similar interests and objectives.

- *Compulsory meetings.* It's essential that members of the club are able to be present in all meetings. When there are resolutions that need to be made about ongoing investments and forthcoming investments, it's imperative that all members are part of the resolution process. If the club resolution is held up because some members don't show up frequently, the undertakings of the investment group are put at risk. The rules and structure of the club will be very important. All aspects need to be discussed.

- *Stock investment resolutions.* Before purchasing or selling any stock, it will be necessary that all members of the investment club are part of the study of these stocks and part of the final resolution.

- *Internet access.* Members of the investment group will require computers with Internet access such that they can monitor the market from their homes and so that they can communicate with other members on a regular basis. The significance of good communication among members of the group cannot be stressed enough.

- *Responsibility checkpoints.* It will be essential that the investment club put checkpoints in place that account for all investments, returns, losses, and other capital concerns. These checkpoints should be readily accessible by all members of the club to read at point in time.

An investment club should run effortlessly with a great amount of consistency and assurance among its members. When all members of the club anticipate and meet similar requirements, everyone works together in a manner that encourages triumph and, optimistically, some productivity.

DIFFERENT CATEGORIES OF INVESTORS

There are diverse techniques and kinds of investors that are in the stock market. Stakeholders use the stock market to shape their investment portfolio such that they can see long-term revenue that takes place over a long period of time.

Someone who just uses the stock market to make money fast for a short period of time is known as a "trader". Members of an investment club fall into the first group: they are in the investment market for the long haul.

There are various categories of investors that use diverse techniques to explore the market and the market conditions.

These three techniques of exploring the market are:

- *Technical scrutiny.* This technique of scrutiny is used by a "momentum" investor. Technical scrutiny looks at the price variations that transpire in the stock market. The investor bases the resolution to purchase or sell on what he feels the price will do next.

- *Fundamental scrutiny #1* Fundamental scrutiny is used by the "growth" investor. This form of scrutiny determines if a particular firm is a good investment based on the earnings of the firm, growth trades, and margins of revenue.

- *Fundamental scrutiny #2.* A "value" investor uses this form of examination. This technique of examination is similar to the scrutiny that a growth investor uses but is somewhat diverse. A value investor takes a closer look at those firms in the stock market that have a low value. The investor looks at stocks that are presently low-priced but have the probability to make a good comeback.

Majority of the investment clubs use the fundamental technique of scrutiny to make most of their investing resolutions. Technical examination and physical examination should also be used when needed. Sometimes you may have to visit a firm physically and make inquiries.

If you cannot visit the firm, a phone call or text message may work for you.

They find firms that are listed on the stock market that display good growth, revenue, and earnings but that are still economical to purchase and have not yet attained their potential. The tendency of marijuana stocks has been to sell off in the summer and rise in the winter.

Members of the investment club purchase this stock and hold on to it for a number of years as long as the details, as listed before, continue to hold strong. This form of investment tactic is known as "buy and hold". In new industries, purchasing great companies early can make a big difference when you buy and hold. We will look at the best marijuana companies and etf's later in the book.

GETTING A MARIJUANA INVESTMENT CLUB STARTED

U.S. Hemp-Based Products Sales, 2012-2022e

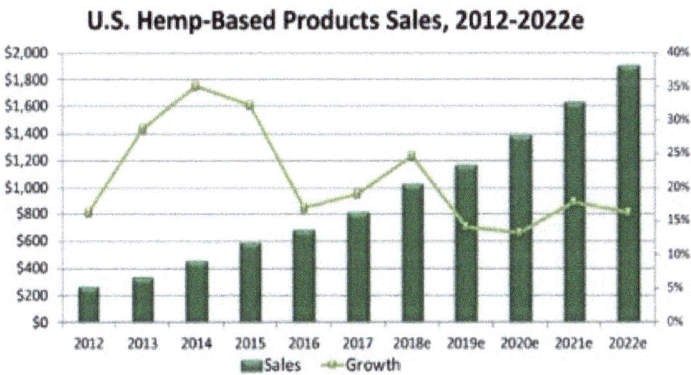

Source: *Hemp Business Journal* estimates ($ mil., consumer sales)

As you can clearly see, sales are expected to skyrocket in the coming years and this sector will be a great place to be.

Step 1 – Finding Members Today

Once you have the basic facts assembled together regarding why you should start an investment club, and the necessities that members should have, you are set to take the first step towards formally starting your investment club.

You will have to look for members with a risk tolerance to join your club and you can accomplish this in various ways.

If you have one or two associates who have presented a common interest in the stock market or bond market, you can ask them to join your investment club.

You can get other individuals who are interested in joining in your club by advertising in the newspaper or by putting posters on public bulletin boards.

The major thing to note is that you want to draw people who are interested in learning more regarding the stock market as they invest small amounts of capital.

You should not be too worried if most of the people who have expressed the desire in joining your club are all new to the stock market. In fact, this can be a noble thing that your club comprises individuals who have no actual knowledge in the market. At times, their views can be paramount.

Individuals who have previous experience with the stock market may quickly become discouraged and have their persistence tested with amateurs.

Don't be too concerned about being part of a group of individuals that have no knowledge as there are many resources that are available to assist you learn about investing and the course that you need to follow. Growing your financial knowledge is a primary objective of the marijuana investment club.

Before your first meeting with those individuals interested in joining your investment group, you should make available the facts regarding the club. This comprises letting them know what the club is going to be about and how it should function.

Step 2 – The First Scheduled Meeting

When you get together for the first time, there are a number of things that you will need to debate. Let all the members have the chance to add their contribution into the meeting so that all ideas are taken into account.

Ensure that you give more time for this first meeting such that you have adequate time to discuss all of the following concerns:

- *Mutual interest of the stock market.* Ensure that all the members you have a common interest in starting

31

a marijuana investment club. You want to ensure that you are all on the same page about the club. Let them know in advance that you are investing in a new sector that can offer explosive growth as well as major disappointments.

- *Organization.* Discuss the particular facts of how the club is going to be run. At this moment, you can discuss about the objectives of your club management and how you plan to accomplish this organization.

- *Obligation.* All members should be aware of the obligation level that is necessary to be part of an investing club. This confirming that there is a significance to be a member of the club will give anybody who has doubts an opportunity to decline being a member. Starting or joining a marijuana investment club requires a time commitment.

- *Reading and study material.* There should be a list of material about investing that everybody should read to become more conversant with investing methods and descriptions. In the next meeting, members can start to talk about the finer ideas of investing.

- *Approach of investing.* There should be a joint pact about what investing strategy your club is going to center on. Take a poll if the group is divided regarding any investing matters. As this is still the first meeting, any member that is in serious disagreement regarding the resolutions made at this first meeting has an opportunity to decline being a member. Members should come to an agreement that this is long term obligation and if their objective is to get wealthy within a year or two and then leave the club, it goes against the objective of the marijuana investment club. It's a marathon not a sprint.

- *Monthly contribution.* Members should come to a joint pact on how much money they are each going to contribute every month. Remember that you can make modifications to the least amount rule at a future date. A lot of clubs start out with small contributions of anywhere from $25 to $60 dollars.

33

This capital is used for the club's managerial fees as well as input into the investment fund.

The first meeting is a good way to clear the air and start to create some basic rules for the way your investment club is going to be run and what your objectives are going to be.

You will want to ensure that most of the members are thinking the same way. Everybody should be in the same chapter and if possible the same page.

There are some other managerial concerns that you will want to talk about at your first meeting. These managerial issues include:

- *Meeting times.* The club should decide on (1) the days and time that you are going to meet (many investment clubs get together once every month), (2) the place that you are going to meet, (3) the length of the meetings (most meetings last about two to three hours), (4) the administrative plan that each meeting is going to take.

- *Number of members.* Decide on the scope of the investment club. Research indicates that an ideal size for an investment club is roughly 10 to 15 members. When you limit the size of the club to this many members you're still small enough to hold meetings in member's homes. All members and officers must have confidence to speak up at meetings. They also need the humility to recognize when wrong and have the mental agility to change as you learn and evolve.

- *Meeting place.* You might want to come up with alternative meeting places, such as local library or café, to use as a substitute meeting place.

- *Club title.* You will want to come up with a title for your investment club. You don't have to make this resolution on your first meeting; but members should come to the next meeting prepared with a number of ideas to share for a club title.

Once you have decided on all of the above concerns, you are ready for your second meeting where you will be taking care of more of the finer ideas of investing, such as legal specifics and tax matters.

To prepare for some of the more comprehensive facts and resolutions that you are going to have to make, you should allocate responsibilities to members to come ready to the next meeting with the following material and data:

- partnership contract forms-trust is also voluntary

- information for organizing a mission statement

- banking details

- legal forms, such as tax details

- information about establishing a partnership

- local by-laws about investing

- broker details

- accounting information

- re-investing shares

- investing information and articles

- a list of current members, including phone numbers and addresses

When emphasis is put on all of the above particulars your investment club will be off to a good start.

Assigning responsibilities is a good way to include all members and to get errands accomplished in a timely manner.

Vote on major and minor issues so everyone has a voice

Step 3 - Election of Officers

When the time comes for the second meeting of your investment club, you will want to settle on some resolutions that have to do with the way your club is run and structured.

You will want to define some of the tasks that need to be accomplished and what officers are going to be nominated to handle those tasks.

All positions should be openly defined such that members can be nominated to these positions. Remember that all members of the club will have duties but when you select officers, you will have some positions filled where members have a specific responsibility and task.

Many investment clubs will have the following officials:

- *President.* The president can also be referred to as the presiding partner. The president determines when the next meeting is going to be held (commonly done with a joint vote but made formal by the president), chairs the meetings, and plans events (commonly done with a joint decision by other members).

- *Vice president.* The vice president can also be referred to as the assistant presiding partner. The vice president assumes management when the president is absent or needs assistance with presidential responsibilities. The vice president is frequently the one who plans some of the enlightening information that is provided to the club at meetings.

- *Treasurer.* The treasurer is also referred to as the financial partner. The treasurer deals with the brokerage company and does the purchasing and the selling of stock. The treasurer also is accountable for keeping precise records of the financial assets of the club, the financial contributions of each of the members, and any other records that concern themselves with capitals and financial issues.

- *Secretary.* The secretary is also referred to as the recording partner. The secretary is accountable for keeping the proceedings of each meeting. The secretary also informs other members of any forthcoming meetings. If a member fails to show up in a meeting, the secretary is the one who passes the proceedings of the last meeting to the absent member so that everybody is kept up to date of all meeting resolutions.

- *Education officer.* Most clubs have what is referred to as an education officer. This member of the club is in charge of planning educational events such as guest speakers, reading materials, field expeditions, and exhibitions that have to do with investing.

When you select members to fill the above positions, you are basically ensuring that your club is run in an ordered and well-organized way. The education officer will have their hands full since the marijuana sector is shifting with lots of sectors and sub-sectors. Having a look at these sectors early will give your club a head start in this high risk undertaking.

U.S. Hemp-Based Products Sales, 2012-2022e

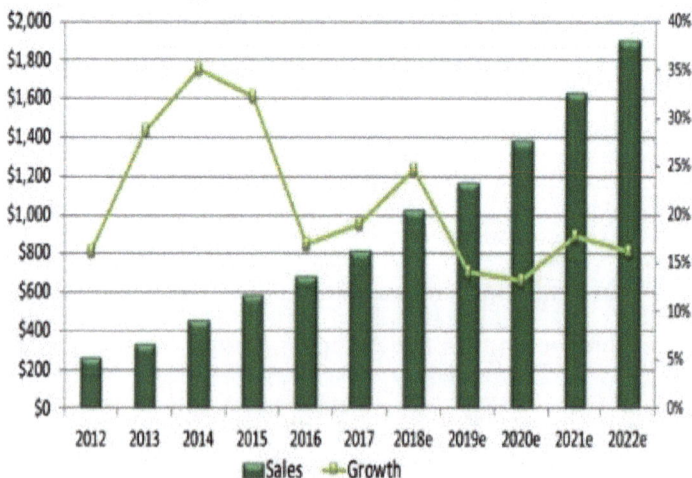

Source: *Hemp Business Journal* estimates ($ mil., consumer sales)

In a new industry like marijuana, it may not be a bad idea if you had a legislative officer who briefed the members on new rules and laws

Guidelines for the Second Meeting

After accomplishing your first meeting, you will want to ensure that some things have been finalized for the second meeting.

These duties include:

- *Registering your marijuana investment clubs corporate entity with the state.* This includes the title of your investment club. When the paperwork returns, the recently nominated Secretary of your investment club should ensure that the paperwork is filed and that members of the club can access to the information.

- *Tax ID Number.* This is the time to file the information that is essential to acquire a Tax ID Number. The recently selected treasurer will now be in a position to open up a banking checking account for the club as well open a brokerage account. If your investment club has not decided on what brokerage to use, this responsibility will have to be postponed to a later date.

- *Education program.* The vice president, or the education officer, should be organizing the first education program that you are going to commence learning.

- *Accounting.* The recently selected treasurer should have the accounting system set up before the second meeting is held.

- *Software programs.* If your investment club is going to use other forms of software to keep track of stocks, returns, expenditures, and other managerial information, the newly appointed secretary can acquire this software and have it set up. Remember that if more than one member of your club is going to use the software program on their computer, you will have to buy several copies of the software or purchase several licenses for more than one user. Most clubs have passwords for the President, Vice-President and Treasurer.

- *Copies of last proceedings.* The secretary should be sure to have copies of the proceedings from the last meeting accessible to all members of the club. This is so that all the members, whether or not they are nominated, feel that they are a part of the whole investment club.

- *Original copies.* All original copies of formal documents should be kept by the secretary in a secure place. This comprises any registration documents, member information, stock acquisitions, and any other official records that need to be secured.

Your investment club should also be well ready as possible for the second meeting. If you notice that one or two members from the first meeting have dropped out, but you still wish to maintain the numbers of your association, you should welcome any new members to the second meeting.

Step 4 – The Business Model

Your investment club will have to choose the type of entity you are going to implement for commercial purposes. You will have to agree whether you are going to be a corporation, a general organization, or limited liability company. Each of these corporate models has their own benefits and shortcomings.

- *Corporation.* Many investment clubs will shun becoming a corporation. This is because corporations are chargeable trade bodies that involve well-informed accounting expertise to make them run efficiently and in accordance with government guidelines. A corporation in general means a lot of paperwork. This paperwork can be evaded by selecting another commercial model for the purpose of running an investment club.

- *General organization.* This type of business model involves less paperwork and awareness regarding taxes and other financial concerns. Majority of the investment clubs select a general partnership as their choice of a trade body. A general partnership has minimal paperwork and expenses associated with it since the taxes are distributed to each partner's tax returns. This form of business model will allow you achieve what you need to do to run your investment club with the minimum amount of tax impact.

- *Limited liability corporations.* This form of business model is much like the general partnership but it gives individual members of your investment club a bit more obligation security. Remember that this form of trade entity can be costly and will require more paperwork.

Members of your investment club will have to choose which of the above business models works best for your club.

You will have to make a choice one way or the other since instituting a trade entity is a necessity for tax purposes.

Step 5 – Registration

The location of your investment club will be a determining factor regarding the requirements for the registration of your club.

The requirements for registration will differ depending on what state or province you reside in. You will have to inquire from your local government about the requirements.

If you reside in the United States, you can get in touch with the Office of the Secretary of State for more information regarding the registration of your investment club.

The United States will allocate what is referred to as a "Federal Tax ID Number" to your investment club. You will be required to use this ID number on all your excise returns.

You will also require the ID number when dealing with a brokerage company and your bank when opening accounts for your investment club.

To acquire a Federal Tax ID Number, you have to get an IRS Form SS-4, which can be acquired at any local library, or you can get in touch with the IRS website directly on the Internet to get a copy at IRS.GOV

The process and procedure of getting a government ID number for tax purposes will differ depending on what country of your residence. The above information is exclusive to the United States.

No matter what state you reside, it's important that you request your Tax ID Number as soon as you can to avoid delay. A delay could imply a delay in your investing plan.

MISSION STATEMENT

You will have to come up with a suitable mission statement for your investment club. This is not something that you have to do immediately but within a few months of your startup you will need to have your mission statement in place.

A mission statement for your investment club is a modest way for you to stay dedicated and mindful of the objectives that you have set for your investment club. Your mission statement will describe plainly how your investment club will be structured and how you are going to accomplish your objectives. You will need to note down your mission statement and ensure that all members of the club, and any future members, have a copy of the mission statement.

EDUCATIONAL PROGRAM

When your marijuana investment club is just starting out you will need to find informative material that is going to give all the members an outline of how investment woks. If you agree as a club that you want to expand on all types of marijuana stocks, you will require the most recent industry facts from meetings and seminars.

As time goes by, and members become more knowledgeable and well-informed about investing, you will need to increase the power of your educational program. It does not matter where you are in the level of learning material that you are looking at, you will need to have a definite strategy about what you desire to learn.

Start out slow with your learning program and build up. Take time to have conferences that talk about what each member knows about investing and what they want to learn regarding the course. Keep records of what members wish to learn so that you always have ideas for learning programs in the future.

At times, you might want to invite a guest speaker to your conferences to give you first hand knowledge of the investing world. This is an ideal way to acquire facts that you can dynamically adopt in your own investment club. Proficient investors can give you an outline of their own investing strategies and guidance. This can give your club some great new concepts to invest your monthly contributions, and the more concepts that you have, the more investment incentives you will have.

Finding a Broker

Your investment club will need to find an investment agent to work with. You can appoint someone to come up with some agent selections and then take a final poll for your resolution.

Most investment clubs will use a full-time agent who directs them and gives guidance at the occasional meeting. If you do not want to use an agent on a full-time basis, you can use what is referred to as a discount agent.

A discount agent will give you some comprehensive facts regarding stocks but will not offer you guidance on what to sell or purchase. Using a discount agent appears to be the more common choice since the purpose of the investment club is to make your own choices about what stocks you will be dealing with.

When you use a discount agent you will not have to pay a huge commission to a full time agent. Your club will have to take a poll and agree upon the interest of the majority. You may also want to consider using the services of an online agent.

Online discount agents will have small commissions that can be an advantage to your club when it comes to handling your finances. On average, an online agent will be up to $8 or less per deal.

How to Find a Discount Broker

If your investment club has concluded that it's in your best interest to use a discount agent, you will need to know how to find one. It will not matter what discount agent you choose to use as long as your club is permitted to select your own stocks.

There is a great deal of competition when it comes to discount agents, so you will be able to get some good deals in agent fees if you take the time to look for them. Your investment club should appoint one or two members to find the best discount agents that they can find, both on the Internet and locally.

There are a few things that you should remember when you are looking for a discount agent:

- Customer service that the agent offers

- Charges

- Additional incentives to hire the agent

The charges that you have to pay the discount agent will normally be fairly low. You will be able to see many discount agents offering you their services both locally and on the Internet.

Though, most times, selecting the discount agent with the lowest charges means that you may be sacrificing some customer service for this lower fee. You will have to choose if you want to trade low price for client service.

If you are considering about employing your discount agent from the Internet, there are certain things that you should take note of.

Online agents commonly fall into one of three categories:

- *Very economical.* If your investment club is preparing on doing a lot of purchasing and selling in the stock market, you will want to consider using a very economical agent for your dealings. Most of these low-cost agents charge anywhere from $4 to $10 per transaction. The era of the FREE TRADE

BROKER has come. Do your exploration and find some to equate.

- *Moderately priced.* The mid range fee that these agents charge is anywhere from $10 to $29 per transaction.

- *Expensive.* Agents that charge a high fee per transaction regularly offer you the best customer service so the fee might be worth it to your investment club. You will get the chance to work with an agent that provides you great service. These agents normally charge anywhere from $29 to $49 per transaction.

When you are looking for an agent and centering your choice on customer service and the way the website works, you will need to take some time looking at the agent's website. They are not all the same.

You will need to ensure that the website is easy to use and easy to navigate and is up most of the time.

You will want to know what type of client service the agent offers. You will soon be able to make your choice regarding client service after you conduct your first transaction with the agent.

Ensure that you find out if there are any other incentives offered that make you want to hire the agent.

Other incentives that online agents provide that can be of help to your marijuana investment club include:

- Informative books and materials to purchase at a discounted rate or to read online.

- air miles for your air mile program

- unrestricted Internet access

- a discount on your first transaction or request for FREE TRADES

Your investment club should not make its resolution regarding the agent to use based on the additional incentives that are provided.

Take your time to decide what agent you will finally hire. It's one of the most essential first resolutions the firm will make. If it narrows down to two or three agents that have interested the members of your investment club, you will have to elect and have a majority ruling on the agent.

Always remember that you can change agents at any time that you wish if you are not contented with the first agent that you have been working with.

INVESTMENT SOFTWARE

There are various types of software that are available for your investment club to make things, such as investment choices and accounting practices, easier and more efficient for you to complete. Good software is a necessity. This should be a priority in any investment club.

It will be to your advantage to have some of the members of your investment club have diverse types of software on their home computer such that you can make more informed resolutions about where you wish to invest.

- *Stock analyzer.* There are diverse types of software available that will assist you to evaluate the stocks that you are interested in and keeping an eye on.

- *Accounting software.* You will need to have software for accounting purposes so that you can monitor all your finances and create reports for all members of your investment club to have for their records. You will also need to use your accounting software to monitor cash trades, member dealings, and security transactions.

- *Portfolio record keeper.* This type of software will monitor your portfolio. It will monitor information such as investment charges and dealings, your acquisitions and trades, member transactions, and stock market fluxes for your stocks.

There are a number of other different types of software that you can use to help your investment club to function efficiently and so that you can monitor your returns and expenditures. This will keep members on the same page.

EASY ACCOUNTING FOR INVESTMENT CLUBS-SOFTWARE

https://6e570bx8odf7hy6adps2nh4cwq.hop.clickbank.net/

Resources for Marijuana Investment Clubs

The following links are some great resources that your investment club should take advantage of to make the most out of your investing experience. There are numerous resources that you can google and find free

US Securities and Exchange Commission (SEC)

This website gives you some basic information about investment club guidelines.

Securities and Exchange Commission

Office of Investor Education and Assistance

450 Fifth Street, N.W.

Washington, D.C. 20549-0213

http://www.sec.gov/investor/pubs/invclub.htm

Investment Calculators

These tools can assist you to calculate a range of information that includes the future value and present value of stocks.

http://www.investopedia.com/calculator/

BEST MARIJUANA STOCKS & ETF'S

The following are some of the most dynamic marijuana stocks in the industry and how to read the stock information.

If your marijuana investment club is thinking about making its first investment, you will need to keep these stocks and etf's in mind.

Please note that all information should be checked to confirm the precision of stock prices currently.

Stocks can decrease or increase in a matter of hours so any stock price information that you acquire should constantly be confirmed. This is why an agent is essential for your investment club. You require someone who can keep a constant eye on the stock market and the stocks that you are looking at.

Though, the reason you have started an investment club is so that you can learn how to observe the stock market on your own and do your own investing.

Your club should take every chance that it can to learn how to observe your own stocks such that you are not depending on any external sources.

Canopy Growth Corporation CGC This Canadian firm is involved with the production, distribution and sale of cannabis products all over the world.

Stock Activity

Last Price 33.50

52 Week High 59.25

52 Week Low 24.46

Average Daily Volume (13wk) 4.3m

50 Day Moving Average 39.08

200 Day Moving Average 43.60

Innovative Industrial Properties. IIPR This American company deals with industrial real estate. They are a marijuana real estate investment trust (REIT)

Stock Activity

Last Price 106.95

52 Week High 139.53

52 Week Low 31.61

Average Daily Volume (13wk) 528k

50 Day Moving Average 119.35

200 Day Moving Average 87.10

GW Pharmaceutical. GWPH This American company is a biopharmeutical company focusing on discovering, developing and commercializing cannabinoid prescription medications using extracts derived from the cannabis plant.

Stock Activity

Last Price 165.91

52 Week High 196.00

52 Week Low 90.14

Average Daily Volume (13wk) 370k

50 Day Moving Average 170.80

200 Day Moving Average 164.36

GREAT MARIJUANA STOCKS TO STUDY

Company	Symbol	Market
Charlotte's Web	CWBHF/CWEB	OTC/Canada
Cronos Group	CRON	NASDAQ
Tilray Inc	TLRY	NASDAQ
Aurora Cannabis	ACB	NYSE

GREAT MARIJUANA ETF'S (Electronic Trading Funds) To STUDY

Company	Symbol	Market
Cambria Cannabis ETF	TOKE	NYSE
Amplify Seymour ETF	CNBS	NYSE
Spinnaker ETF	THCX	NYSE
Advisor SH Pure Cannabis	YOLO	NYSE

Two Amazon.Com Books With Plenty Of Stocks To Select From

STOCK SYMBOLS

This is an outline of the letter symbols that classify stocks according to a variety of details. Each security has a specific letter that has been allocated to it to make it unique and so that you can easily identify it.

- A - Class A

- B - Class B

- C - Issuer qualification exemptions

- D - New

- E - Delinquent in necessary filings with the SEC

- F - Foreign

- G - First convertible bond

- H - Second convertible bond, same company

- I - Third convertible bond, same company

- J - Voting

- K - Nonvoting

- L - Miscellaneous situations, such as depository receipts, stubs, Warrants and units

- M - Fourth preferred, same company

- N - Third preferred, same company

- O - Second preferred, same company

- P - First preferred, same company

- Q - Bankruptcy proceedings

- R - Rights

- S - Shares of beneficial interest

- T - With warrants or with rights

- U - Units

- V - When-issued and when-distributed

- W - Warrants

- Y - ADR (American Depository Receipts)

- Z - Miscellaneous situations such as depository receipts, stubs, additional warrants, and units

After you have been investing for a short time and reading the stock market, you will become conversant with these symbols.

GLOSSARY OF INVESTMENT TERMS

The following investment terms will help give your investment club a simple introduction into the language of investing.

The more that you comprehend about the world of investing the more you'll enjoy your investment club, increase your literacy and have a good time.

ALL OR NONE (AON) Order

A clause to either a purchase or a sell order which instructs the agent to either fill the order in its totality or to fill none at all, the client will not accept a partial accomplishment (only 300 shares out of an order for 1000).

APPRECIATION

Appreciation is the increase in the worth of an asset

ASKED PRICE

The minimum price that anyone has will sell their security for at any given time. In over-the-counter stocks, the "ask" is the best estimated price at which a Market Maker is willing to sell a stock.

AT-THE-MONEY

At the money option is where the strike (exercise) price is exactly the same with the trading price of the underlying security.

BID PRICE

The maximum price anyone has stated that he wants to pay for a security at a given time.

BROKER

(1) A person or companies that charge a fee or commission for performing purchase and sell orders submitted by another individual or company. (2) The role of a brokerage company when it acts as a broker for a client and charges the client for its services.

CALL OPTION

An option agreement that gives the holder the right to buy, and places upon the commitment to sell, a stated number of dividends of the underlying stock at the given strike price on or before the expiration date of the agreement.

CAPITAL

Accrued money or goods used to generate revenue

COMMERCIAL PAPER

Commercial Paper is Short-term loans with maturities ranging from 2 to 270 days that are made to banks and companies.

COMMODITY

Commodities are bulk goods such as metals, food products and grains which have the price determined by competitive tenders and bargains.

COMMON STOCK

Common stock is an equity security position that symbolizes possession in a company.

CUSIP NUMBER

A unique 9-digit number code for a given category of security (i.e.: Microsoft common stock or Acorn International Fund). CUSIP stands for the Committee on Uniformed Security Identification Procedures.

DAY ORDER

An order to purchase or sell which, if not effected, expires at the end of the trading day it was entered.

LIMIT ORDER

A limit order is direction given to an agent to sell or purchase stocks at a particular price or better.

DO NOT REDUCE (DNR)

Stipulation to order that instructs the agent not to cut the limit price on buy-limit and sell-stop orders on the record date of a cash share.

EXCHANGE

An exchange is any business, association or group of individuals that retains or offers a marketplace in which securities can be purchased and sold. An exchange does not have to have a physical place of business and a number of electronic exchanges do business.

NASDAQ National Market Securities

The NASDAQ National Market comprises of over 3,000 firms that have a national or global stockholder base, have applied for listing, meet strict financial requirements and agree to particular business governance ideals. To list initially, firms are required to have substantial net tangible assets or functional revenue, a minimum public float of 500,000 dividends, at least 400 stockholders, and a bid price of at least $5.

NASDAQ Small Cap Market Securities

The NASDAQ Small Cap Market comprises of over 3,300 firms that want the aid of Market Makers and have applied for listing and meet particular financial requirements. They do over 1.8 billion trades every day! Once a firm is sanctioned and listed on this market, Market Makers are able to quote and trade the firm's securities through a sophisticated electronic trading and surveillance system.

PENNY STOCKS

Penny Stocks are low price stocks trading in the over-the-counter market. Normally Wall Street and financial markets denote to firms trading below five dollars a share as penny stocks. Most marijuana stocks will be under five dollars a share.

TRADING AUTHORIZATION

Document permitting power-of-attorney rights to a broker of the account holder(s). You will find downloadable forms for both Limited Trading Authorization and Full Trading Authorization in the Industry Forms Download area.

For the Road

Starting your own marijuana investment club for pleasure and revenue is easy when you follow the information and strategies as outlined in this book.

It does not matter whether you are an amateur investor just starting out, or a more skilled investor that wants to expand into more investments, there are individuals out there who share your interests and objectives.

When you are part of an investment group, you will have the benefit of learning more about investing in the stock market combined with the pleasure of spending time with people who have a mutual objective: to become more experienced about investing and have fun doing it.

There are many books that you can purchase, and places on the Internet, that outline the information and data that you need to invest successfully and profitably.

Investing does not have to be an scary experience but should be something that you have fun doing.

After you use the steps and information in this book about starting a marijuana investment club you'll be on your way to investing in the stock market. THANK YOU VERY MUCH FOR YOUR SUPPORT! MAY GOD BLESS YOU!

If you found any value in this book, please do the honor of leaving a short book review at Amazon.com. Thank you very much for your support. Other books your club may enjoy that can be found on Amazon.com include:

GREAT AUDIO BOOKS

ON

MARIJUANA - 30 DAYS FREE

INVESTING IN MEDICAL AND RECREATIONAL CANNABIS, Buy in Before, during or After Legalization: https://www.audible.com/pd/Investing-in-Medical-and-Recreational-Cannabis-Audiobook/B07GNTK1Z4?asin=B07GNTK1Z4

MAKE MONEY ONLINE WITH CANNABIS STOCKS: https://www.audible.com/pd/Make-Money-Online-with-Cannabis-Stocks-Audiobook/B07G1QF839?asin=B07G1QF839

ROMISING MEDICAL MARIJUANA AND CBD TREATMENTS: https://www.audible.com/pd/Promising-Marijuana-and-CBD-Medical-Treatments-Audiobook/B07GHQFHWZ?asin=B07GHQFHWZ

THE LARGEST INDOOR AND OUTDOOR MARIJUANA FARMS IN THE WORLD:

https://www.audible.com/pd/The-Largest-Indoor-and-Outdoor-Marijuana-Farms-in-the-World-Audiobook/B07GRDT8JP?asin=B07GRDT8JP

THE AFRICAN MARIJUANA GOLDMINE, Rich Mineral Soil Meets Wall Street:

https://www.audible.com/pd/The-African-Marijuana-Goldmine-Rich-Mineral-Soil-Meets-Wall-Street-Audiobook/B07GNTRTTL?asin=B07GNTRTTL

HAVE GREAT MEETINGS AND MAKE MILLIONS!!!!